I0017751

How to become a

UI Designer

A practical career guide

By Wendy Zhou

About this book

Who is this book for?

This book is for anyone who wants to learn UI design and begin working with it!

What will you learn?

You will learn about how to land your first UI design job, including which skills to learn, what software you can use, and how to create your own design portfolio.

In addition, this book contains other tips and insights such as the pros and cons of employment versus freelancing, the different earning potentials for various specialties, and different ways of finding design inspiration and improving your skills.

Words from the author

While there have been many books written on the theoretical aspects of design, there are few that offer hands-on practical advice on *how* to practically go about starting a career in UI design and land your first job. This is the gap that this book aims to fill.

Since this book is more practically geared, it has been written from my own experiences and everything I've read and learned on my own journey. While I have made efforts to keep things as objective as possible, inevitably, some information will be subjective.

To balance this subjectivity, you'll find a long list of other resources and theoretical books that you can check out in the last chapter (10. References & Book Recommendations).

I hope that this book can help you and answer many of your questions!

Introduction

UI design is probably one of the most exciting fields today because it shapes our entire digitalized world. The work of UI Designers is all around us, from morning to night.

UI design is the design of the alarm clock you interact with, first thing in the morning. It's also the interface design of all our social media apps, the smart system in our cars, and the ticket payment system in public transportation.

Close to every single individual today comes in contact with UI design, during all parts of their day. It's anytime we interact with our smartphones, our computers, or any other smart devices.

More increasingly, UI design is being implemented in physical public spaces all over the world. For example to unlock buildings, buy tickets, pay for food in restaurants, and even to check in at hospitals.

For those who want to help create and shape those interactions, both current and future ones, UI design is a great way to do it.

At its core, UI design is an interdisciplinary skill between technology, human psychology, and aesthetics. It is also that combination of skills that makes the work creative, intellectually challenging, and varied.

As technology advances, even more ways of human-technology interactions will be invented, and those technologies and interactions will need to be designed as well. So, it is still not too late at all to begin learning UI design.

In truth, UI design can be an art, it can be experimented with, and it can be broadened in the scope of what's possible. Much like in fashion, sound technology, and programming. Find what parts of it excite you the most, and dive into that.

Table of contents

What is UI Design?

Defining differences between UI, UX, and front-end

1. What is UI Design?

UI stands for *User Interface*, which is the space where humans (also called users) interact with technology. This "space" can be a website, mobile app, or some other type of digital interface that you can click, tap, swipe, or talk to.

UI Design is the design of such interfaces. It concerns for example the design of websites, mobile apps, VR environments, and AR. It is the design of everything you see and interact with when using a digital product or app.

UI is also closely related. and sometimes even synonymous, with the terms UX design, product design, interaction design, and front-end design - depending on who you're talking to.

1.1. UI Design & UX Design

As mentioned, UI (user interface) design is closely related to UX (user experience) design - which is the design of how a user *experiences* a product or design.

The user experience can be both positive and negative. A user can for example experience a design as enjoyable if everything works as expected. But, if the user instead gets frustrated or irriterad, that would lead to a negative user experience.

It is the job of a UX Designer to design and shape products to be enjoyable, efficient, and useful for the user. UX design is therefor highly human-centered, and always considers the users wants and needs.

Generally, a UX Designer works with the research part of the design process, such as interviewing users and defining user needs and wants, performing usability tests, creating user journeys and personas, as well as drawing up the information architecture.

UI design is generally referred to the latter parts of the design process, including creating polished visual designs and mockups, prototyping and animations, as well as the graphic design parts regarding color palettes, font choices, and illustrations.

But since UI and UX design are so closely related, UI design cannot be entirely separated from UX design. UI design is therefor also deeply rooted in human-centered design. And, in order to create designs that are enjoyable, efficient, and helpful, both UI and UX design must coexist.

For example, an app can look great and aesthetically pleasing, visually, but if the user is unable to do what they want with it, because of confusing navigation or missing key features, then they won't return to use it again.

Likewise, if a design has great UX design, but lacks in the department of visual design, it can make the entire design or product look outdated, untrustworthy, and cheap.

Thus, the best combination is to always apply both user experience design and user interface design into any project.

1.1.1. Combined roles

In reality, many companies and teams are looking for multifaceted designers who can do both UI and UX design, as well as know some front end. These combined roles are often called UX/UI Designer, Product Designer, or just Designer.

Many also do not know the difference between various design roles, so they combine the roles. So, some companies may market a job opening as looking for a "UX Designer", but in reality, they may be looking for a highly skilled visual designer.

The title "Digital Product Designer" has also become very popular in recent years. As the name suggests, Product Designers work with the entire product cycle, including research, visual design, business thinking, and sometimes even coding. The focus is on the entire product and strategy.

To find out what a company is truly looking for, read the job descriptions carefully and identify which skills and methodologies they mention.

- For more research-based roles you will find keywords such as usability tests, information architecture, design thinking, and interviewing
- For more visual roles you will find keywords such as pixel-perfect mockups, visual communication, and graphic design principles

- For combined roles, you will find: a combination of research skills, visual skills, and knowledge of HTML and CSS

In job interviews, you can also ask about how the design process usually works in the company, and which design methods they commonly use.

The combined information of all the above-mentioned aspects will help you distinguish what type of work you will actually be doing, and if it fits your personal desires.

1.1.2. The expected skill sets

While many companies may combine various design roles or confuse them with each other, there are some that do know what they are looking for. And for those that do, there are some common distinctions between what's expected from a UI design role versus a UX design one.

Let's take a closer look at the differences between the roles of a "UX Researcher" - which will be our example for a UX design role, and the role of a "Visual Designer" - which will be our example for a UI design role.

UX Researcher

A typical UX Researcher performs research and usability tests, designs information architecture, creates personas, and maps out potential user journeys. These are examples of methods that a pure Visual Designer, usually is *not* expected to do.

Further, job positions as UX Researchers often require a higher academic degree, sometimes even a Ph.D. This is because these types of roles need to perform reliable research, as well as may require theoretical knowledge about psychology, human factors, cognitive science, and other similar subjects.

Visual Designers

In contrast, Visual UI Designers are in general expected to have somewhat of an artistic talent or a strong eye for aesthetics. In fact, many who pivot into visual UI design work come from a graphic design or illustration background.

When companies advertise for a visual design role, they are generally looking for someone who can create gorgeous, polished, and aesthetically pleasing mockups. They may even already have a UX Researcher on the team and may be specifically looking for someone to take over the wireframes after research is done.

In the job application process for a visual design role, the applicant's visual skills may be much more important than their academic or theoretical background. Employers might look for polished, gorgeous, and artistic screenshots and mockups, rather than long research-based documents.

Larger organizations

In larger organizations, such as Google and Facebook, specialized roles are more common. For example, the jobs of a UX Researcher, Visual Designer, Interaction Designer, and UX Writer are often separate.

How design roles may look like

- UX Researchers perform research, create the overall layout of the design, and perform usability tests

- Visual Designers build on top of the work of UX Researchers, creating the visuals such as adding a coherent color palette, choosing typography, and creating gorgeous mockups and illustrations
- Interaction Designers create the prototyping - sometimes even in code - and all the micro animations for interactions
- UX Writers polish text content and make it readable

Smaller organizations

In smaller organizations and startups, it is more common to hire generalists, who can do combined roles such as a UX/UI Designer or Product Designer.

This is mostly because smaller organizations may not have enough financial resources to hire multiple specialized roles, or simply haven't reached that level of design maturity yet.

Besides, smaller organizations must distribute their resources to other contributions as well such as marketing, development, sales, and customer support.

Can you be great at both?

There have been many discussions in the design community for years about whether a person can be both a great UX Designer and UI Designer simultaneously.

Some say that no one can be an expert on everything, while others believe that it is fully possible for a human to learn multiple skill sets and be great at many things at once.

There is no clear winner to the argument yet. However, trends in the market show that there is an ever-increasing amount of companies that choose to hire so-called unicorns, generalists, UX/ UI Designers, and Product Designers.

Personally, I believe that any person who is ambitious, driven, and self-disciplined can learn both with the right resources. UX and UI design are not that far apart, although one lies a bit more toward logic and the other toward artistry.

Further, there is a concept in economics, called human capital which states that a person's human capital is the sum of our abilities and resources. The more skills and abilities you have and build, the more your human capital increases.

According to the concept of human capital, it goes to reason that adding more valuable skills only makes you more valuable. It doesn't make you *less* capable of other things. This applies to developing skills in both UX research and visual design.

Of course, a person's natural talents may dictate how good one can get at a faster rate, but that does not mean someone without talent cannot work hard to improve to the same level.

There are many people in the world who are good at multiple things and enjoy many sides of life throughout life. For example, corporate workers who love the free art scene, writers who paint, boxers who enjoy reading and drinking tea, and so on.

As technology advances, with improved AI, increasing global competition, and fast-moving markets, we may all need to become generalists and flexible in expanding our skill sets.

In the future, we might not have any choice *but* to be good at multiple things at once.

1.1.3. Usability

Usability is traditionally more related to UX than UI, but even if you are a visual designer, understanding usability is essential when designing user interfaces.

Usability stands for how effectively, efficiently, and satisfactorily a user can utilize a design or product. It's evaluated by asking the question of whether the user can perform the desired action and obtain the desired results.

Designing with usability starts with a user-centered approach, which means always keeping the user and their experience in mind. At every step of the way, emphasize with the users and reflect on how they might feel, act, and think.

This means not only focusing on designing visually pleasing interfaces, but to design interfaces that are valuable in terms of functionality, features, processes, and feedback.

The usability of a product or interface design is best assessed and improved through usability tests, which often fall into the tasks of a UX Researcher.

However, I'd highly recommend every UI Designer also learn the skills of usability testing or at least usability evaluation. Great UI designs are always dependent on also having great UX design. Thus, UI is never fully separable from UX.

Learn more about usability in chapter [4.2 Usability](#).

1.2. UI & Front-End Development

User interfaces such as websites and apps need to be developed in code, which is where front-end and back-end developers enter the picture.

Front-end developers create the visible parts of user interfaces using HTML, CSS, and Javascript, which is what you will be designing for as a UI Designer.

Back-end developers create the non-visible parts of user interfaces (e.g. fetching and sending data to databases and security checks that run in the background when logging in). This is not something UI designers typically need to dive into.

For UI Designers, front-end development is therefore the relevant part of development, and it's more closely related than you might think.

1.2.1. Do UI Designers need to know how to code?

The answer is no, a UI Designer typically does not need to be able to write functional code.

However, you do need a solid basic understanding of front-end development and how interfaces are built. You need to at least know what types of components front-end developers work with and how they manipulate them.

If you do not have enough knowledge about front-end development, you will not be able to judge the feasibility of the features and designs that you create.

It will result in the risk that you design things that are not technically reasonable or functional.

1.2.2. UI Designers that code

Knowing the basics of front-end development is also crucial to be able to communicate with the rest of your team.

You'll be able to answer questions developers may have about the design, as well as use the correct terminologies when discussing different solutions.

Needless to say, if you are not able to do any of these things, you'll be severely restricted in your role and ability to function well with others.

UI Designers that understand the technical aspects of what they're designing and building are of course more well-equipped and more valuable to any team.

This means that if you also learn the basics of code, you will be able to take on more jobs, work in a bigger variety of teams, as well as demand more pay.

In summary, with a combination of design and development skills you are able to:

- Communicate better with everyone on the team, especially developers
- Design more technically feasible interfaces
- Create more efficient Design Systems
- Be able to contribute to building components if needed

The value of someone who's in the intersection of both design and code is so prominent that there are even roles specific to this intersection such as UI Engineers or UI Developers.

So, even if most of the time, a designer is not *required* to contribute to actual code, being able to do so makes you more valuable.

1.2.3. The consequence of not knowing code

The risk of not having enough technical understanding may be more important than the benefits.

Bad business & reputation

If you do not understand what you're designing, you may very well end up designing interfaces that are not technically feasible, which is a big waste of time and resources.

It costs companies a lot of money to hire skilled workers, and designing UIs that can't be created in a timely manner within budget is simply bad business.

It could also affect your reputation as a designer in the long run, especially if you want to build a brand or business of your own.

Social status & impact

As mentioned, you may also experience problems communicating with the rest of the team which hinders overall productivity and affects the perceived value of the designer. You may not be able to explain your design choices or speak up to contribute.

It may result in the design being lower on the hierarchy of importance and influence, which could lead you into a position where you are not able to do anything impactful with your work. And being in that position is not fun.

Job competition

Other designers, who do have a better understanding of front-end development, may also be chosen before you when applying to the same jobs or getting higher pay for the same type of job.

With experience

The above-mentioned problems may not appear as a junior UI designer in a large team of more senior decision-makers, but they will probably become apparent at some point in your working life.

Most designers sooner or later realize the benefits that come from understanding basic front-end development and thus decide to learn it.

It is therefore recommended, even if it's not always required, that UI Designers have a basic understanding of HTML, CSS, and Javascript.

I would recommend you learn the basics, and who knows, perhaps you'll even enjoy it! It can be very satisfying to have the ability to create what you've designed, without needing the help of someone else.

Either way, as a UI Designer, be prepared to be around and interact with front-end code and developers plenty during your total work life.

1.2.4. In teams

Even if UX Design, UI Design, and Front-End Development can be seen as separate roles, they are often so intertwined that they need to work in collaboration and cross-functionally to produce the best results.

As mentioned above, depending on the size of the organization, UI Designers can be expected to possess a great variety of skills.

It is possible to have a purely visual role, but most likely you are expected to either learn UI and UX design, or UI and front-end development.

The smaller the company or team, the more likely you are to be expected to perform multiple roles. In most cases, it will also be highly appreciated if you can and are willing to contribute with more skills.

1.3 Generalists & Specialists

As you develop your skills as a designer, you will likely at some point need to choose how to focus your energy. Will you want to *broaden* your skill set (generalist) or *niche* down (specialist)?

Some designers and developers work across all sections of product development. They are called *generalists* or *unicorns*. Others specialize in one specific area, called *specialists*.

You can specialize in any niche area you want such as specifically creating dark mode UIs, mobile apps, websites, interactive components, creating Design Systems, or animations.

You can also broaden your skill set as much as you want. UI design related to UX design, interaction design, front-end development, back-end development, project management, digital marketing, content creation, writing, graphic design, and more.

The advantage of being a specialist is that you can become an expert in your specific niche, being able to do that thing better than anyone else. The advantage of being a generalist is that you can find connections between various specializations, and draw upon each of their strengths and come up with innovative approaches.

Both ways of developing one's skills are valuable but will fit differently into different organizations and stages of product development, as well as your own personality.

It is of course hard to know what to do right at the beginning of your career, so my advice is to try to learn as many basics as you can in different areas, and then experiment. You will with time notice where your natural talents and interests lie.

With experience, you will also more likely come in contact with all areas of product and business development. This will probably teach you things about various different skill sets whether you do it on purpose or not.

So, for example, do focus on purely UI design in the beginning, but with every project and team you're working with, keep an open mind towards the other aspects of product development.

1.3.1. T-shaped skill set

Designers are in general often also encouraged to develop a "T"-shaped set of skills.

The long top line of the T represents having a broad spectrum of general skills in many areas such as UI, UX, interaction design, front-end, and strategy.

The long middle line of the T represents specialized knowledge and skill in some areas, such as Design Systems, animation, interaction, project management, usability tests, or CSS.

The specific shape of your "T" may develop naturally as you gain more experience and learn your natural talents or interests. As a beginner, it is encouraged to try a lot of different areas and gain as much knowledge as possible, before specializing.

1.3.2. In companies

Generalists and specialists fit differently into different organization sizes and in different stages of product development because those states need different sets of skills.

Smaller organizations – Generalists

When working with startups, smaller companies, and early-stage product development, a generalist may be more fitting due to financial constraints and efficiency.

A generalist may be able to perform multiple roles at once and be more flexible. It is cheaper for smaller companies to hire one person to do the jobs of multiple people, which unfortunately also could mean extra stress for the designer.

Smaller companies may also need to move faster and by removing middle hands and trimming down the number of team members, a product can be developed faster and more efficiently.

The benefit of working as a generalist early on is that you get to try out and dabble in lots of different areas, which teaches you what you enjoy. You may also get to do more impactful work.

Larger organizations – Specialists

In contrast, in larger organizations, and with more established products, specialists may fit better for fine-tuning improvements and more funding.

Larger and more well-funded companies have more resources to hire experts in different areas. They can also afford to spend money to improve specific parts of a product, without rushing, compared to smaller companies with a tighter budget.

The advantage of entering in a more specialized role in a big company is that you often get proper mentorship and they may even have a proper learning process for junior designers.

The disadvantage is that your work may be such a small part of the whole, that you may not feel like you are doing anything impactful or visible.

1.3.3. Generalist vs specialist when freelancing

If you're aiming to become a freelancer or self-employed, you may still want to consider if you want to be a generalist or specialist. Both have their advantages and disadvantages.

Being a generalist as a freelancer means that you have the skills to take on more possible projects. For example, if you're having a hard time finding work within UX research, you can instead take a UI design project.

If you are a specialist, however, you can become well-known for your specific type of niche. This can make you become the "go-to" person for this type of project, which allows you to charge more.

Being a specialist is therefore one of the key components to developing a strong personal brand as an independent creative professional. However, it may also limit the variety of projects you may take on.

Most designers start off as generalists and then niche down. This process can depend on factors such as where your talents lie, what you enjoy the most, and what is most in demand.

2. Software & Tools

There are many design software available for UI design, which has been specially made to help designers create mockups and prototypes.

UI design software is based on vector graphics, which is a form of computer graphics based on geometric shapes such as lines, points, and curves as opposed to drawn pixels.

Vector graphics are important because UIs are built upon such geometric shapes, and you'll often need to export components that need to be re-sizeable without losing quality.

As a beginner, the exact tool you learn isn't very important, since they are all fairly similar. Once you have mastered one, you will be able to quickly learn another.

However, it can be beneficial to learn tools and software that are popular. Popular software has more available tutorials, and guides, as well as may save learning time when you begin working with a company that uses the same software.

2.1. Most Popular Design Software

Two of the most popular and recommended UI design software are **Figma** and **Sketch**. They are all fairly easy to learn and you can create wireframes, mockups, and prototypes with all of them.

Figma

Figma is a very collaborative software, designed for teamwork, allowing multiple people to interact with a document simultaneously. For example, you can see other people's live actions, leave comments and reply to them, as well as play games and chat inside files.

In addition, it's fully cloud-based, meaning that you can access it from any device with the internet, and it also has an offline mode. However, it does work best on a desktop.

Figma also allows for plenty of plugins made by companies and individual contributors, community files, and features such as auto-layouts and resizing.

Sketch

Sketch is a solid design program that has been an industry staple for a long time. It has plenty of functions offered by Figma, and you will have no problems creating designs with it.

However, the catch is that Sketch is only available on Mac for editing, which can be restrictive. But, if you want to make a point of supporting indie companies, Sketch can be a great choice as Figma is owned by Adobe.

More advanced tools

There are also other more specialized tools, such as Framer and Principal that are more geared towards complex and detailed animations and prototyping, as well as others dedicated to niches such as 3D modeling.

More specialized software often has a steeper learning curve, which you do not need to directly burden yourself with from the start. Therefore, I'd recommend beginners to first learn easier ones, and then get familiar with additional tools as one's skills advance.

2.1.1. Recommendation

I personally recommend beginners to start with **Figma,** since it's free for personal use! Figma also offers a lot of helpful guides and tutorials to get you started.

There is also a very active community amongst Figma users, that share plenty of free files, tips, tricks, and tutorials with each other on sites such as Twitter. This online community can be a great deal of fun for anyone who may not be surrounded by many designers in their physical environment.

In addition, the fact that Figma is entirely cloud-based is great! It will make it easy for you to design more frequently and from different locations and situations in your life. I personally also believe that this is the future way of working with digital design in a remote climate.

Since Figma is so popular, learning it can also increase your chances of more easily fitting into various companies and organizations that also use it. This can lower the threshold for getting your first job or being able to create your first professional project.

2.2. Learn How to Create UI Components

When you begin learning how to create designs in your chosen software, it can be helpful to start with the basics - common shapes, visual effects, and components.

Almost all UI design and front-end development are built with a recurring number of components. If you master these basic components and features, you'll soon be able to recreate any design you might come across.

Basic UI components to learn how to create:
- **Shapes** such as rectangles, circles, and triangles
- **Fine adjustments to shapes** such as adding border-radius (rounded corners)
- **Grouping and layering** of elements and frames - For example combining a square and a circle to create a new shape
- Adding **colors** that can be solid or different types of gradients (combinations of colors that are gradually overlapping)
- Changing the **opacity** of components. Lower contrast to make something less visually distinct, and vice versa
- Adding **shadows** with different colors, strengths, and opacity. You may also add multiple shadows on top of each other to create the effect of various elevations and floating

- Adding **grids** as guidelines to help you see where to place UI components for consistency and aesthetics
- Adding **auto-layouts** to groups of elements to get consistent amounts of padding, margin, and other repeated spacing
- Various **frame and screen sizes** to simulate different devices (mobile, tablet, desktop, and tv)
- Adding **prototyping** - practice thinking about the entire user journey and the experience from going from one part of the design to another

With enough experience with various UI design components, you will be able to start getting creative with how you combine the components you've seen or made in the past.

While you're at it, you might as well also try learning some common keyboard shortcuts. I won't go through them here since different software uses different shortcuts, but I'd recommend you learn how to shortcut:

- Creating a group of elements
- Select multiple items in one mouse drag
- Deleting one or multiple elements
- Zooming in and out
- Scrolling vertically or horizontally
- Various ways of changing multiple elements at once

How to Design User Interfaces
The Design Process & Methods

3. How To Design User Interfaces

Apart from knowing how to use software and create UI components, you'll need to learn how to take an idea or concept and translate it into the appropriate UI design.

You'll also need to know how to evaluate if your design is a good solution to the idea, concept, or aim. This is the hard part, and a skill that can only be improved by experience and practice.

In the design process, there are a variety of methods and processes that you can use. These have been developed across multiple design fields for different purposes.

In this chapter, we are going to dive into the different methods you can utilize when designing a user interface, their pros and cons, and when you could benefit from incorporating them.

A user interface can be designed through various methods. Ideally, and in most textbooks, designers are taught to strategically go through a long list of methodologies and systems to achieve the best outcome.

In reality, most designers are working under restrictions due to factors beyond their control and often deviate from best-practice processes.

So, don't feel the burden of needing to go through every single step fully in each project, but learn them so that you have them in your arsenal of methods going forward.

3.1. The Design Process & Methods

Before we dive into the different common UI design processes and methods, here's an overview of them.

1. Project brief
2. Competitive analysis
3. Finding inspiration
4. Visual guidelines
5. Brainstorming & conceptual models
6. Low-fidelity sketches
7. High-fidelity mockups
8. Prototypes
9. Accessibility
10. Content & Copy
11. Evaluation & feedback
12. Presentation & argumentation
13. Designer-developer handoff

Note again, that in real life, a design process is seldom done in a strictly systematic way, but more often moves organically through various methods.

Reminder: Great UI cannot be done without UX design

You will notice that in order to create the best UI designs, you have to consider usability, and product strategy, as well as adopt some research thinking. As a beginner, you don't need to be an expert in all areas, but to create better designs, you have to have a holistic approach.

Limiting factors

All projects have limiting factors that affect what you can and cannot do, even if you want to. These factors can be things such as rushed deadlines, limited resources, as well as soft limitations such as stakeholders not seeing the value of certain methods.

Such limitations often force designers to pick out and prioritize the most essential methods for a project, which may lead to a more organic, but less systematic, design process.

Not following a strict methodology isn't necessarily bad, as long as you have the needed knowledge to be able to choose wisely between what methods you *do* incorporate.

Because of these common restrictions, a lot of designers choose to create what is called a personal or passion project. These are projects that you choose for yourself, and that you create in your own time as side projects, unrestricted by many of the constraints you'd otherwise encounter in a corporate environment.

I'd advise you to create your own projects, especially in the beginning in order to practice all the different methods and to start building your portfolio.

3.1.1. Project brief

Design projects start off with a project brief. A project brief is a summary of what a project will entail, to make sure that everyone is on the same page.

Define the project's purpose

Define why this project is being done, what problems it's trying to solve, and what the goals are. What are the expectations for the project and how is the end design or product envisioned?

Goals & objectives

What is the goal of the product or design, both for the benefit of the company/organization and the user or the world? Amongst those goals, which ones are the most important ones?

In addition, are there important KPIs (Key Performance Indicators) that one is creating the design for? What features and functionalities should the design contain?

Target user group or audience

Who are the audience or target user group? Which personas or groups of people are we going to empathize with while designing? What does that target user group wants, need, and enjoy?

This can be a company's ideal customers or the group of people an organization is aiming to help. The information can be found by talking to the intended users themselves, creating digital or physical surveys and interviews, and speaking with people who know the target user group well.

Constraints & ethics

What technical, financial, or other constraints are there? What assumptions do we make about the market, customers, and restrictions?

These restrictions can take the form of a lack of available competencies to carry out certain tasks, a lack of finances, local and international laws and regulations, as well as cultural and social stigmas. Be sensitive to how the outer world might react to the design, and what the unintended consequences may be, and reflect on ethical and moral aspects.

Project duration

How long is this project expected to take? What deadlines or milestones are we working with?

Project scope & deliverables

What form is the end product or design expected to be in? Be specific in determining what the deliverable will be.

Are you expected to only showcase ideas and concepts, pixel-perfect mockups and prototypes, or perhaps even developed finished websites and apps?

The expectations should be well established before the work begins. If you are unable to deliver what is asked, you can still do the project but may need to bring in external assistance and expertise. This will affect the budget and possibly the timeline of the deadlines.

Resources

What resources, internal and external, do we need, have, or need to get? This can be anything from employees, external contractors, paid-for services, memberships, networks, physical and digital tools, and so forth.

It can be a good idea to gather all available competencies and resources in a document so that when, and if, you need it during various points of the project, you can quickly find it.

3.1.2. Competitive analysis & research

Before sketching out your first ideas and concepts, it can be a good idea to first find inspiration as well as see what types of similar products and designs already exist. This will help save you time, and energy, and kickstart the creative process.

When you know what you are to design, according to the project brief, you can now do some research and dig into what other similar products and designs you can find on the internet.

There is almost always someone or many, who have done the same thing already. Find these other designs through search engines, similar businesses, asking people, and browsing design social media such as Dribbble, Behance, or other sites that collect designs.

It can be especially useful to look at your top competitors in the market and reflect over:

- What features, functionalities, and conceptual models do other similar products have, and do they seem to work?
- Look at the reviews and see what other products and designs get praised for, and what feedback they get from their users
- What weaknesses of your competitors can you learn from and do even better?

- What strengths of your competitors can you also include in your own design, and improve on even more?

By using this method, you can make sure that the product or design that you're creating is *at least* as good as the other ones on the market, and hopefully even better. This is one-way innovation and improvements can be born.

This foundational step is very important, and the ability to do such analysis distinguishes how much impact your designs can make.

You, as a designer, will be able to contribute much more *value* to the entire product or design if you learn to analyze competitors and the market.

3.1.3. Finding inspiration

Once you've got an idea of what features your design will have, the overall conceptual idea, as well as a good grasp of competitors, you can start gathering inspiration.

Inspiration can both be visual (e.g. screenshots of competitive products or conceptual designs found on the internet) or text (e.g. value propositions, visions, and goals).

Inspiration does not need to come from similar products or services, it can also be purely visual inspiration from other great designers, artists, illustrators, or even nature.

Gather the inspiration you find either physically or digitally so that you have an overview of the different points of reference you can begin working from. This will speed up your creative process immensely as well as get your creative mindset going.

The inspiration you gather is meant to guide you in the design process, and the point is not to copy other people's creations straight off, but to gather enough base for you to spin off from, and build on top of.

Our brains are creative, yes, but they are also limited. By being inspired by other works, you're essentially feeding your brain with new ideas, perspectives, and reference points.

3.1.4. Visual guidelines & design systems

Does the company or organization you design for have a set of visual guidelines or a design system? If yes, you should learn how to work with them, and if not, you may need to create one yourself.

Following guidelines may hinder how visually creative you can get with each project, but it creates consistency in the design, creates a stronger brand, as well as speeds up the design process, and can lower costs.

Visual guidelines

Visual guidelines are tied to branding, and it's guidelines about how a company or brand wants to portray itself to others.

By following visual guidelines, brands can have a coherent and consistent identity, similar to how a person can have a strong identity. Having a strong identity can help a product or company gain visibility as well as build continuous trust and returning users.

For example, Apple has a strong visual identity and guidelines that make it instantly recognizable. You might glance at someone's Home Screen on the phone and immediately recognize it as an iPhone because you recognize the layout, font, and UI components - it's the same with their packaging.

Visual guidelines contain files and guidelines such as logos and how they should be used, color palettes, fonts and font pairings, guidelines for graphic design and print work, and so on.

Design system

Design systems are a specific type of visual guidelines aimed specifically towards UI design, and may not contain any guidelines regarding physical print work and graphic design.

A typical design system contains things such as logos, color palettes, layout guides, UI components (e.g. buttons, tabs, controls, input field, dropdowns, shadows, menus, search bars, and cards), guidelines for states such as error messages and feedback indicators, icons, and illustrations.

Design systems may be created using programs such as Figma and Sketch, which allows you to create libraries of UI components that can be dragged and dropped into new projects. The same components can be created in a code library by developers.

Using drag-and-drop UI components saves time for each new project since you don't need to redesign each component from the ground up. In addition, developers can also reuse previous code, knowing that the components will look and act the same each time.

Over time, using an efficient and well-established Design System and component library saves both time, money, and energy.

At the start of a project

If the company or organization you're working with has visual guidelines, make sure to include them in your design as well. In most cases, you are not only designing according to your own personal tastes but in harmony with the overall bigger brand and vision.

It's important that you find out about these visual guidelines before diving into creating any designs since you may need to relate your design to earlier guidelines. If you do it too late, you may need to go back later and re-do work, which is a waste of time and resources.

If they do not have any guidelines, however, you may need to create them before or during the project as a part of the deliverable, depending on the scope of the project.

You could explain to stakeholders what a visual style guide is and ask them if they want to invest some time and budget into creating one. You might get an additional fun project to work on.

If there are no prior guidelines

If you have no prior guidelines to work with, you can easily create a basic one by going through and analyzing earlier designs and graphics.

Put together the material you find from previous designs and identify frequently used visual details such as a color palette, common fonts, and pairings, frequently used border-radius, and the overall visual tone. You can then apply these common elements to the new design to make it fit in better with the overall branding.

Note! If you are creating a proper design system from scratch, do invest adequate time and energy into making it good and efficient.

Create design systems in collaboration with developers and stakeholders so that the guidelines are technically feasible, as well as set up in a way that is usable by others as well.

3.1.5. Brainstorming & conceptual models

Once it's time to start creating the actual visual UI design, it's easiest to start off by brainstorming.

Brainstorming is a method where you allow your brain to flow freely, coming up and sketching down any and all ideas you may find relevant.

This stage is all about idea generation, allowing your brain to be creative and come up with ideas, and not stopping too much to reflect on details. Do not judge your ideas at this point.

The ability to come up with good conceptual models and ideas improve with time. A seasoned designer may be able to do it without any external assistance, but as a beginner, it's very helpful to start from the inspiration you gathered earlier.

So don't be afraid to look at other people's designs to start with.

Step-by-step

1. Get a pen and paper

Get yourself a piece of paper and a pen, or use digital means, since the main point is to sketch out as many relevant ideas and concepts from your mind as you can.

Doing this first step by hand, on pen and paper, without attention to detail is helpful since it's a low investment - meaning that you won't be too attached by a quick sketch or scribbles.

So, do *not* sketch your first ideas in detail or invest any time in drawing shadows, putting energy into making every line perfectly straight, or making any pretty illustrations.

If you do this step with too much attention to details or by creating each idea in a pixel-perfect mockup, you will have a much harder time deleting the bad ones.

This step is just to get ideas out of your mind, and into something a bit more concrete.

2. Mindset of non-judgment

Get in the mindset of not judging anything you sketch down. Let go of any pressure that the first idea you put down needs to be good.

Think the opposite, your first few ideas probably will *not* be the best, but you just need to get them out of the way so that better ones can come through.

Allow your mind to flow freely and create concept after concept until you can't think of any more good concepts.

3. Group features and functionalities

Look at the list of features and functionalities you set up at the beginning in the project brief. How do different features and functionalities relate to each other, which ones should be grouped together on the same page or even be combined into one component?

4. Imagine the user journey

Think about what the user journey will be like. For example, which functionalities and contents should be shown at different steps of the user's journey?

Not all features and content may need or should be cramped into one long page, perhaps they ought to be separated and linked with each other through multiple screens, steps, or sections. How would these screens be linked?

5. Plan the information architecture

Think about how different pages or screens should relate to each other in an architectural plane. How will the menus look and which items should they contain? Which pages are most important, and how will the landing or start page reflect that?

6. Use gathered inspiration

Look at the inspiration you gathered earlier, and start analyzing them. What features do you think are good in them and which are relevant to your project? Is there anything in the inspiration that you can add to your own project?

7. Evaluate ideas

When you have come up with multiple sketches and concepts, you can begin to evaluate them. Evaluate each idea by writing the pros (+), cons (-), and possible improvements for each one.

From your evaluations, go back and strike out the worst ones, and continue improving the better ones. You might find that you can add and blend ideas from multiple concepts.

If you don't like any of your ideas, start over until you have something to go from.

Following conventions

Remember, there is nothing wrong with following conventions and creating things in a way that users are already familiar with. Following conventions will lessen the learning curve for new users as well as minimize possible confusion.

In the absolute majority of cases, it is more important to design and create something that is highly *usable* and *efficient*, rather than entirely ground-breaking and innovative.

Innovation is good, but if users cannot use the design because it's too different, it can lead to feelings of frustration, struggle, and confusion. And if users experience negative emotions while using the design, it means that they're having a negative user experience.

3.1.6. Low-fidelity sketches

When you have your conceptual model down of how the design or product will be laid out and what it will contain, you can start creating your first low-fidelity sketches.

Low-fidelity wireframes do not need to look perfect or polished, the details are not important. Do not spend any considerate amount of time perfecting shadows, adding colors, or creating perfect shapes.

You can even work entirely in greyscale and do it by hand with paper and pen.

The focus of low-fi sketches and wireframes is to illustrate:

- The general layout and structure
- The contents
- Functionalities

What are low-fidelity mockups good for?

Low-fidelity sketches and wireframes are great for visualizing multiple ideas fast and help with brainstorming through different options. It can also help you explore ideas without being too attached to them.

Visualization of ideas is also needed in order to be able to evaluate them and show them to others. It is difficult to present a design idea to others using only words, hence it's better to show it to them visually.

These fast sketches and wireframes are also great because it allows you to iterate them without wasting too much time. If you're going to change large parts of the design multiple times, it's unnecessary to invest too much time into fixing details that will be removed anyway.

Skipping low-fi sketches

In some cases, you may not need to begin with low-fi sketches, such as if you're only improving an already existing design with a Design System or if you're working under time pressure. You'll need to judge for yourself if it makes sense first to start with sketches or if you want to jump into creating mockups right away.

3.1.7. High-fidelity mockups

In this step, you start doing what most people think of as UI design, which is the detailed and visual design of the user interface.

What are high-fidelity mockups?

High-fidelity mockups are high-quality and polished versions of the design, including all details such as specific colors, shadows, interactions, and illustrations.

These mockups have all the content placed out where it should be, exactly how they look and acts as a detailed blueprint for what the developers will create using code.

Depending on the project and need, the high-fidelity mockup can vary in complexity. For example, in the deliverable, you may need to include high-fidelity mockups including:

- Mockups for different screen sizes: desktop, tablet, mobile, TV
- Copywriting and UX writing
- Detailed UI illustrations
- Interaction design, prototyping, and animation

3.1.8. Prototypes

Once the high-fidelity mockups are finished, or close to being finished, you can begin mapping out interactions. This is called prototyping.

Prototypes are interactive versions of the design, simulating how the finished product, after coding, should look and behave. A prototype is still only a vector based, not yet implemented in code.

For example, you may have designed:
- One screen with two buttons to "Login" or "Sign up"
- One screen for what you see once you've logged in
- One screen for filling in your information to create an account/sign up

Prototyping is when you link the components so that clicking on either buttons "Login" or "Signup" on the first page, takes you to the relevant following page.

3.1.9. Accessibility

Designing with accessibility in mind is important to make the internet an inclusive space.

It means designing user interfaces that can be used by a broad number of people including those who might have disabilities.

Examples of edge user cases that can be forgotten are users with bad or non-existent eyesight, people with difficulties using a mouse with precision, and different environmental factors such as using an application in the sun or in a dark room.

There are official government websites with UX guidelines for accessibility, such as accessibility.digital.gov by the U.S. General Services Administration.

Some of the key questions to ask yourself when designing with accessibility in mind are:

- Is there enough contrast between the text and background color? This can be checked with WebAIM's Color Contrast Checker or plugins in design software
- Is the font size large enough to be comfortably read? In general, a minimum of 16px is needed for paragraph text
- Is the line height comfortable for reading?
- Is the typeface/font choice clear and legible?
- Are the headings communicating hierarchy effectively?

- Can you add icons to give helpful visual cues?
- If you have text over an image, is it readable or do you need to add a colored overlay or blur the background image to make the text more legible?
- Have form fields been properly labeled and do they support navigation with tabbing?
- Do form fields have clear and defined boundaries?
- Are error states highly visible and specific?
- Are touch targets big enough? In general, they should be at least 48px
- Can you navigate well using the tab key on the keyboard?

3.1.10. Content & copy

Text is just as important as visuals when it comes to digital products and design. Text can be used to set the tone (branding), sell (copywriting), clarify and explain (UX Writing), and help products gain visibility in search engines (SEO).

If you want to be a designer that can make a bigger impact through design, then it is absolutely necessary to understand the value of the text.

In most cases, UI Designers are not expected to be experts in forming textual content, but there may come occasions when you'll be the only one dealing with all the content.

Having a solid understanding of the value of copywriting, UX writing, and SEO, will without a doubt affect the way you design content.

It can show up in the way you understand business goals, where you place important elements, and how you decide to name buttons and other elements.

You don't need to be an expert in all three skills, but understanding how the skills impact the end results can guide you to ask the right questions.

For example:

- Knowledge of **copywriting** can help you decide where to place a call-to-action button to improve conversions. It can also help you design better landing pages and product pages.
- Knowledge of **UX Writing** can help you with naming buttons, tabs, and menu items to make them as clear as possible. It can also help you decide what information to include in error messages and where to place them.
- Knowledge of **SEO** can help you use headings (H1, H2, H3, etc.) in the right way. It can also help you in deciding what data to include in strings to make individual pages rank higher on search engines.

Copywriting

Copywriting is the design of text to sell in marketing or advertisement.

In terms of UI design, copywriting is most prominent in landing pages or product pages where the company wants the user to take an action such as creating an account, buying a product, or subscribing to something.

Small tweaks in the copy of UI components such as call-to-action buttons, and their placement on the page, can have big impacts on conversion rates.

There are UI designers who specialize in the intersection between copywriting and UI design, working exclusively with these types of design tweaks.

There's a lot of money to be made both for companies and for independent creatives with a specialized combination of these skills.

UX Writing

UX writing is used for designing text in a way that improves user experience.

This includes for example making sure there's a friendly tone, using words that are easy to understand, as well as writing from a user-centered perspective.

In UI design, skills within UX writing can be applied to
- Making sure that error messages and warnings are clear, easily understandable, and delivered with a good tone
- Writing text for buttons, tabs, menu items, and hyperlinks that are self-explanatory and fit user's expectations
- Reformatting highly technical content in simpler terms

SEO

SEO stands for *Search Engine Optimization* and determines how visible a website, application, or product will be in search engines such as Google.

A website with search-engine-optimized content will rank higher on search results, meaning that it will show up further up in the list of search results.

Websites that rank higher get more traffic, users, and potential customers. For companies, this means more income and sales. This is the part where content design meets marketing, and a knowledge of both is important to create impactful designs.

In UI design, SEO knowledge can be applied to
- Using headings (H1, H2, H3) in the right way. For example in an article, H1 is the main title and there is only one per page, H2 is for headings, H3 for subheadings, and so forth.
- Making sure that the keywords that you want the page to rank for are drizzled in the right headings, paragraphs, page titles, and other components.
- Structuring the URL of a website, such as what you name subpages, and make sure that keywords are in the URL link.
- Making sure that there are separate SEO web pages for content that one wants to rank high for.

- Knowing how to analyze data traffic to identify if design changes can be made to improve user experience. For example, a high bounce rate on a page might mean that users did not get redirected to where they expected. This might be fixed by correcting the text on buttons leading to that page.

3.1.11. Evaluation & feedback

Receiving feedback on your designs and evaluating ideas, both alone and with others, is a crucial part of the design process.

Good design is possible to create alone, but even better designs are most likely created by combining multiple people's competencies. This is the reason why many teams have design feedback sessions and design critiques.

Nevertheless, it can be a real challenge for beginners to gracefully receive critique and feedback. It is not unusual to experience negative feedback as a personal attack on one's skills, competencies, and subjective taste.

To overcome this, one must build a non-fragile ego, lead with humility and openness, as well as build confidence.

These are true soft skills and personal qualities that cannot be taught theoretically, but requires continuous exposure and self-regulation.

Try this:

Be actively *willing* and *encourage* others to give you feedback, early and frequently. Take back the personal perception of control over the situation.

Practice this:

Distance yourself from your work output. Your personal worth is *not* tied to your output. If you must grade yourself, measure yourself instead by the amount of effort you put in and your ability to improve over time and learn.

Think about the design output as "our design" and not "mine". The end product is something created together and *for* the users, so creating the best design together is the priority.

3.1.12. Presentation & argumentation

In order to become a designer who makes an impact, you need to learn how to present your work and argue for what you deem as the best solution.

Presentation is both a matter of communicating your work, as well as persuading stakeholders and other influentials to see the value of your solution and vision.

Good UX & UI design is not only about art or aesthetics, it is about creating something that solves a problem or provides a need for both business and users.

In any case, there are an endless amount of possible solutions, and as a high-level designer, one key skill is the ability to argue for your proposed solution.

Fear of presentation

It is common to feel uncomfortable and afraid of giving presentations and public speaking.

The act of standing on a stage, in front of a group of people, and having all the attention, can leave one feeling exposed and vulnerable.

If you add the possibility of receiving negative feedback on your own work on top of that, the act of presentation may feel even more threatening.

All those fears and worries are valid, but you should not let that stop you, because that's not the only side to presentations.

Benefits of giving presentations

Even though presentations and public speaking may feel daunting, it is still one of *the best* ways of communicating to a large group of people in a way that can truly persuade someone.

Even in this digital era of a multitude of digital means of communication, live vocal and visual communications triumph all when it comes to creating a personal connection, trust, persuasion, and building rapport.

Within any company, group, or organization, your ability to influence and impact is highly dependent on your social standing.

If the people around you do not trust you or have a positive connection with you, you will find yourself in a position of low influential power.

However, if you decide to give frequent and high-quality presentations, you can position yourself as a person of confidence and skill, as well as someone to be considered for decision-making.

Giving a good presentation means you have something to say, you know how to communicate effectively, and you are not afraid to be seen and make connections with your audience. All these are highly important soft skills to learn and develop.

3.1.13. Designer-developer handoff

After research, design, and presentations, your work has possibly been approved to move to the development phase. But your work doesn't stop there. The way you hand over designs to the developers is important as well.

A designer needs to hand over the designs in a way that makes it possible for developers to create them properly in code. This means that they will need more than just static screenshots of the designs.

Developers should be able to inspect the design and get information about details such as specific hex colors as well as paddings and margins. Ideally, they should even be able to interact with the prototypes themselves, so that they can recreate the interaction design as well.

Luckily for us, most modern software has developed specific designer-developer handoff tools. Designer-developer handoff tools allow inspectors to click and inspect details, and some even generate CSS code from the mockups.

For this reason, it's important to choose to work with software from the beginning that has features that are important for aiding designer-developer handoffs.

Before beginning a project, you can also talk directly with the developers about what type of design handoff they will need from you. Knowing this in advance can save a lot of time.

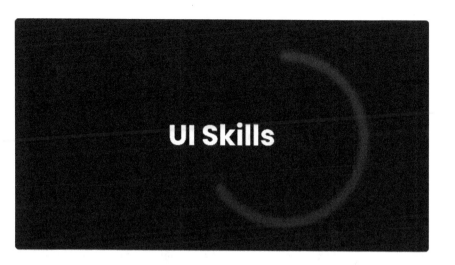

4. Skills & Knowledge

For beginner UI designers, there are basic visual design skills and
usability principles that you need to learn. These skills are what
will make your designs look professional, modern, and enjoyable.

Within visual design principles, UI designers need to have a good
grasp of color, typography, gestalt principles, and knowledge of
how to work with layouts and white space.

Apart from visual skills, good UI Designers also need to be able to
able to work with usability in mind.

4.1 Visual Design Principles

UI Design as mentioned in the introduction, leans toward visual design, as opposed to UX research. The best UI designers are often also great visual designers who often have a great eye for aesthetics.

However, you do not need to be an amazing artist or painter to be good at UI design. Many great UI Designers can't paint gorgeous paintings, but they can create gorgeous UI designs anyway.

Just like any other skill, visual design can be learned and practiced. Many parts of the visual design have even been theorized and can be learned through practical guidelines.

Some of these practices can be to learn some standard uses of padding, font sizes, and go-to colors for backgrounds and texts. Even details such as shadows on UI elements can be copied and pasted as CSS code.

By observing other people's designs you can also learn a lot. Practice noticing what makes something aesthetically pleasing to the eye, and how you can use those principles yourself when creating things.

It can be details such as:

- Layering multiple shadows on top of each other with low opacity and using a grey color or the same color as the main element instead of black
- Always striving for consistency in font sizes, button paddings, and color scheme
- Adding the appropriate whitespace and padding with conscious choice and not just fill up space
- Rounding off corners slightly with border-radius to create softer looks
- Using grids and patterns to make elements properly aligned
- Using paler and lower-opacity versions of main colors to highlight elements
- Choosing fonts that are modern and avoiding fonts that look outdated

Since this book is more of a practical guide on how to start a career in UI design, I won't be going into too much depth in each of these categories. But, I will give you an overview of the most important visual skills that UI Designers work with.

I would advise you to seek out further sources on these design principles and theories on your own. Many of them can be found in the genres of graphic design, illustration, and web design.

4.1.1. Colors

Colors tell us a lot about the identity of a website or app we're using. For example, do the colors give a fun and playful vibe, or is it dark and serious?

Colors are an inevitable part of all visual creations and must be considered in every project. Luckily for us, there are many modern tools that help designers create harmonious color palettes such as coolors.co, and various plugins for design software.

You can also find further inspiration on color combinations and palettes through browsing designs on for example Dribbble or Pinterest.

Classic color theory

You can furthermore learn about color theory, as taught to classical artists. These theories can teach you how to choose harmonious color palettes, as well as what meaning colors have had historically and contextually.

However, since digital designers have a wide variety of helpful tools, it is not necessary per se, to become an expert in color theory in order to create gorgeous UI designs.

Do note though, that there are aspects regarding the psychology of colors, tied to the user's cultural and social concepts. So, keep in mind cultural differences when picking out colors and other visual icons.

How to choose colors for a project

Different colors send out different messages, and that's why it's important to consider the larger vision of the product or design.

Who is the target audience and what is the use context?

- For example, yellow and other bright colors can be more fitting for a website that sells toys to children, while blues and grays may fit better for a bank.

How and when will the product or design be used?

- Dark mode can for example be hard to read while in the sun, while very bright color schemes may be too harsh on the eyes at night.

What image does the company or brand you are designing want to portray?

- For example, a brand may want to seem playful and youthful, or serious and professional. Adjust the colors according to that.

Does the product or company already have an established brand identity?

- Then it's likely that new digital products or verticals for the business should follow the same guidelines, and perhaps you shouldn't come up with your own color palette.

4.1.2. Typography

In UI Design, typography is used to organize the content of an interface in a clear way. This means that text needs to be readable, scalable, scannable, and visually appealing.

Some of the basic things UI designers decide in regard to typography is

- **Font** - For example Times New Roman, Roboto, Lato
- **Typeface** - A family of related fonts
- **Letter and line height** or spacing - The distance between each letter or between lines of text to make it more legible
- **Weight** - The thickness of the font such as thin, regular, and bold
- **Size** - The size of the font such as 16px or 21px

You can find current popular and modern fonts by browsing fonts.google.com, following discussions in forums and social media, as well as inspecting new designs from big companies or popular designers.

In regards to font size, weight, line heights, and so on, there are general guidelines that can be followed.

Quick tips and tricks
- Generally, 16px works well as the base font size for fonts.
- Add more line height to paragraphs to make multiple lines of text more readable.

- Restrict the horizontal length of text lines to create a more comfortable reading experience.
- Make sure there's a clear visual hierarchy that makes more important text visually dominant. Headings should be visibly larger or bolder than paragraph text.
- Adjust text sizes and placement to make the design more scannable. People in general scan through pages as opposed to reading everything carefully from top to bottom.
- Make sure there's enough color contrast between the text and its background color.
- Make a consistent typography scale. Decide the font size for text elements such as p, H1, H2, and H3, and be consistent throughout the design.
- Remove unnecessary filler words unless it improves the user experience, especially for buttons and menu items.

4.1.3. Gestalt principles

In psychology, there are a set of design principles referred to as the **gestalt principles** or laws. These principles are very important in visual design to make parts look like they either belong together - as a group or entity - or to make them look separated.

Gestalt means "unified whole" in German. The gestalt laws are based on psychology and describe how we humans perceive visuals around us, such as seeing patterns and connectedness.

UI Designers can use this knowledge and implement it in digital interface design to make interfaces easier to navigate and use.

For example, we recognize that two buttons that are just on top of each other probably concern the same thing, while content that are further apart probably contain very different types of content.

The 6 gestalt principles are proximity, similarity, figure/ground, continuity, closure, and connectedness. Let's go through each one, with an example of how they can be implemented in UI design.

Proximity

The principle of proximity states that we group elements that are close together, separating them from other elements.

In UI design this can be applied to keeping elements that belong together close such as a primary and secondary button, as well as adding padding between different groups of elements to separate them.

Similarity

The principle of similarity states that things that look similar get grouped together, regardless of their proximity. This similarity can be based on color, size, and shape.

In UI design, elements can be made to look like they belong together by using the same background color, shape, or size.

Elements can further be differentiated by the same principle. For example, make the primary call-to-action button a different color than the secondary button.

Figure and ground

The principle of figure and ground states that our brains distinguish between elements that are considered to be in the foreground and the background.

In UI design, distinguish elements such as a modal pop-up with the rest of the site by adding a blurred background, a shadow, or overlaying everything else with a darker or lighter color.

Continuity

The principle of continuity states that we see things that follow a smooth line as belonging together.

In UI design, elements that are placed in a line after each other naturally draw the eye from one element to the next, such as a horizontal slider or tab.

Closure

The principle or law of closure states that the human brain fills in missing parts to create a whole image. So for example, even if lines or shapes are not closed, our minds can still follow the overall shape.

In UI design, show only a part of an image or button on the edge of a screen to allow users to understand that there's more to see.

In addition, there's the classic trick of making sure content is visible "above the fold", to make it clear that there's more to see if you scroll.

Connectedness

The principle of connectedness says that elements that are connected to each other are perceived as one unit.

In UI design, you can connect elements by adding a colored background or border around them.

4.1.4. Space & Layout

Space

Space in UI design layouts is very important. It's everywhere and you don't think about it until it's missing - that's when you feel that something looks off.

Using space in your layout can improve visual hierarchy, readability, and scannability, and help highlight the most important parts of the design. It's a way to organize the content without adding a bunch of clutter.

Space in digital design is often referred to as "whitespace", and it is created using margins, paddings, line heights, and letter spacings.

When designing with space, keep in mind the gestalt principles we went through in the last chapter. Use space to group or distribute UI components in a way that creates visual hierarchies.

For example, add more space between elements that are more unrelated, and less space between elements that are more related.

This can mean having 46px padding between big sections, 32px padding between the border of the section and its contents, and only 16px between the items inside the sections.

Another easy spacing trick is to add more line height in paragraph texts, which will immediately make it more legible. Not too much, but around 140-170% can often work wonders.

Layout

Space inevitably also affects the layout of a design, so they go hand-in-hand. Layouts are the overall visual structure of the UI components and contents, and also build upon the gestalt principles.

Items that belong together will for example have the same size, color, and shape, and be ordered in the same direction (vertical or horizontal). Different groups of items can be separated by space, color, or size.

When designing the layout, think about the visual journey, and manipulate it in a way that benefits the user. Use size and space to highlight the most important elements.

One traditional way to create consistency in layouts and spacings is to use grids and place out components according to the grid lines.

A newer method is to use functions such as auto-layouts to set an automated amount of padding or margin to groups of elements.

Whichever method you choose, make sure that the spacing is consistent and helps communicate a clear visual hierarchy.

4.2 Usability

Usability in design refers to designing things that are easy to use, efficient, and intuitive.

In order to do so, designers need to emphasize the end user's needs and goals, so that the design and product can meet those needs. It's one of the core components of UX design.

As mentioned, UI design is inseparable from UX design, which means that UI Designers also need to keep usability in mind at all times.

For UI Designers, it's important to design for inclusivity & accessibility, have awareness of cultural differences, and understand some basics of human-technology interaction.

In practice, when designing UIs, usability can take the form of:
- Providing clear buttons and labels
- Creating intuitive navigation
- Following conventions on how things usually function and look
- Making sure there's enough color contrast for the text
- Making sure the text is legible and big enough
- Providing explanations and guides to complex systems
- Placing error messages in the correct places
- Signaling messages with a visual aid such as icons and colors

As you can see, when discussing the topic of usability, it's clear how even visual UI designers need to take usability and user experience in mind. Even if one isn't responsible for UX Research, all of the above considerations are important.

4.3. Learn how a business makes money

It is not talked about much by UI Designers, but the design is not isolated. It is important for designers to understand how the whole of the business functions and how the design value of design is evaluated by most companies.

The reason why a designer benefits from learning this is that can help both you and the company earn more, as well as improve the respect and value of designers in the market. This is especially true for consultants, freelancers, and Product Designers.

The most well-paid UI Designers do not only deal with creating pretty components, they deal with helping businesses reach their goals and improve their income. They use design as a tool for business success, which is why they get paid more.

One way of implementing business knowledge with design is for example by using your skills as a UI Designer to suggest changes in design to better meet KPIs, improve conversion rates, and promote more sales.

If you in the future want to start your own company or design and create your own products or apps, you will without a doubt benefit from having practiced using design as a means to improve revenue. It's a skill best learned by doing.

4.3.1. Design for business needs

In order to learn how companies and products bring in revenue, you need to think in a business-oriented way.

This does not mean that you should abandon human-centered design, which you should not, but rather add another layer of thinking.

For every project you work on, ask the questions of
- What are the main business objectives with this new product or feature?
- What are the different ways we can monetize this product or new feature?
- What are the costs of designing and developing various functionalities, and which should we prioritize to cut costs and increase ROI (return on investment)?
- How are our biggest competitors doing this, and how can we improve our design and product to become even better than theirs?
- How can we present the unique value of this product in marketing and advertising?
- Is there a way we can track the impact of new designs based on the key objectives and KPIs (conversions, revenue, sign-ups)?

Apply your answers and reflections in the UI design, and examine how you can use design to answer those business needs.

If you succeed in this, you can specialize as a Product Designer with strong UI and visual design skills. This is a very valuable skill set to have.

Let's not forget, that of course a gorgeous, useful, efficient, and visually pleasing design also sells.

So, thinking in a business-oriented way doesn't take away the importance and value of great visual and experience design, it just adds even more value.

"I wont to learn how to..." Search

**How to Improve
UI Design Skills**

5. How to improve your UI Design skills

Once you've learned how to use the tool, how to set up a project, how to find inspiration, and how to perform different design methods, you have the basics down.

But now comes the fun part, to practice creating UI designs and becoming more and more skilled. UI design is best learned by doing, observing, creating, and gaining experience.

Experience can come in the form of professional work, but it can also come from your own passion projects, doing daily design challenges, and getting feedback from mentors.

As UI design is a multidisciplinary skill, your continued education can be a combination of both theoretical and practical skills.

You will benefit from learning more about different surrounding skill sets such as UX design, visual design, and front-end development.

I suggest you try out many things in the beginning and observe where you're natural talents and inclinations lie.

What is most enjoyable to you? What do you have a knack for? What puts you in a flow state? And that's the direction you will most likely find joy in pursuing.

5.1. Daily UI Design Challenges

One of the most common beginner challenges you'll find amongst the design community on social media such as Dribbble and Instagram is the Daily Design Challenge.

These challenges are popular within all fields of visual and graphic design and a great way to get started.

As the name implies, the Daily Design Challenges involves creating at least one new UI design per day. This is a great way to get into the habit of creating designs and normalizing that behavior in your daily routine.

Another great benefit of doing Daily Design Challenges is that you can post your results on social media such as Instagram and tag them.

You will find that there are countless other beginners doing the same thing around the entire world, which allows you to find and connect with others learning the same thing. This is the beginning of joining the design community.

There are many pre-made Daily UI Design Challenges that you can follow, where you will get a design prompt each day to follow.

Examples of common challenges can be designing a login and sign-up page, an invoice receipt, a digital ticket, a drop-down menu, or a set of interactive buttons.

Apart from getting into the habit of designing every day, this challenge also exposes you to designing components you may not have chosen yourself.

Similar to working life, where there will be cases when you will need to design things depending on the project needs and not your own preferences.

5.1.1. The 31 challenges

1. Sign Up Form
2. Credit Card Checkout
3. Landing Page
4. Calculator
5. App Icon
6. User Profile
7. Settings
8. 404 Page
9. Music Player
10. Social Share
11. Error/Success
12. E-Commerce Shop
13. Direct Messaging
14. Countdown Timer

15. On/Off Switch

16. Pop Up/Overlay

17. Email Receipt

18. Analytics Chart

19. Leaderboard

20. Location Tracker

21. Dashboard

22. Search

23. Ticket

24. Empty State

25. Dropdown

26. Log in/Sign up

27. Blog Post

28. Calendar

29. Notifications

30. Header Navigation

31. Loading…

Note! While doing this challenge, you can learn a lot from finding inspiration from more skilled designers' work. However, try not to mindlessly copy the inspiration you find, but think about what it is you're doing and why.

Don't just see each daily challenge as a to-do item to check off, but rather see every challenge as an opportunity to learn. By reflecting, thinking, and analyzing, you'll learn ten times more than mindlessly doing.

Ask yourself questions such as:

- Why is a certain color, size, or shape used?
- Are there ways to improve the design you've made? Try making a few different iterations and versions
- What can you learn from this?
- What type of grid, whitespace, padding, or consistency can you identify in the inspiration you're using?
- Can you add more states and interaction designs to your design?
- Try putting your design element in a bigger context

5.2. Copy Work

Copy work is a practice where you find a UI design mockup that is above your current level of skill, and you copy it.

By copying someone else's polished UI designs, you'll need to closely study it, and think about each little detail in order to recreate it.

You'll notice things you might not have picked up otherwise, such as how the colors in the color palette relate to each other, the character and technique used for shadows, consistency in border-radius, and different layouts.

It's similar to how artists learn how to paint by studying and copying masterpieces.

To find work above your level of skill, you can browse design social media such as Dribbble, Behance, and hashtags on Instagram.

You can also choose an application or website that you think has a good design for example Spotify or a polished calendar app.

It's important however to not steal someone else's work. Do not post or share it as your own without giving credit to the original designer.

5.3. Feedback and iterations

One of the best ways to get objective feedback in order to improve is to show your designs to more senior designers.

As a beginner, you won't have enough background experience and knowledge bank to validate your own designs properly. This, senior designers have.

In addition, multiple minds can most likely come up with more ideas and reflections in a shorter amount of time than a singular.

Working together combines the knowledge of different people, and will give you the insight you wouldn't have thought of yourself.

5.4. Mentors

When learning something new, it's always a good idea to have a mentor or multiple, that can help and guide you in your development.

A mentor can be a trusted teacher, a more experienced friend, or an internet connections.

How to find a mentor

There are many ways of finding a mentor. You could for example use specific mentor-student programs that help match mentors with students.

However, the best types of mentor relationships come from authentic interaction. A mentor-student relationship works best when both the mentor and the student get something out of it, such as stimulating and interesting conversations and discussions.

If you ask someone to become your mentor, just to send them a bunch of questions, what is the mentor getting out of it? And why would a great designer spend time investing in such a one-sided relationship?

I'd advise that the best way is to try to learn as much as you can on your own, and create projects around your ideas and knowledge.

Post your projects on the internet, for example on Instagram or Dribbble, and then connect with more senior designers. Engage them in conversations, thought discussions, and ideas. This will create a much more natural relationship.

You could also actively engage in conversations surrounding more senior designers' work, and build relationships that way. Great mentor-student relationships build on shared interests and stimulating exchanges.

5.5. Passion Projects

Design is best learned by doing, and creating your own passion projects is probably one of the most enjoyable ways of learning.

Passion projects are projects that you have chosen yourself, not with the primary purpose of earning money, but with the purpose of creating something you want to create.

It can for example be an app or product idea you've thought about for a long time or something you'd wish existed. So, you create it!

By designing concepts or things you'd like to create, you also develop your sense of product design and innovative thinking. You get to practice how product founders think when coming up with ideas for new products, apps, and systems.

You can of course also include your own projects in your [design portfolio](), which is especially beneficial if you haven't had any real work experience yet. If you do it properly, you'll be able to articulate your design thinking thoroughly through your projects.

Even if you already have some portfolio projects, your additional passion projects may show your personal interests and abilities that you may not have gotten the chance to apply to a paid project yet.

For example, you may dream of working with healthcare products, but only have experience with e-commerce. If you then create great passion projects with healthcare ideas instead, that may be your way into more healthcare-oriented work.

Who knows, perhaps your personal projects may even come to fruition and become real apps, products, and software!

5.1.1. Creating your own design projects

1. Generate an idea

To begin creating your own project, you can use your full imagination! You can allow yourself to dream about what type of app or product you'd want to use yourself.

Is there an app or service that you wish existed?

If you can't come up with anything, try spinning off from existing apps or products that already exist. Perhaps there's a personal finance app, health tracking app, exercise app, or a cool website that you think could be even better? Use that as inspiration for a better version.

Doing personal projects can be very enjoyable, so I'd recommend you to pick an idea that feels exciting for you!

The best part is that you don't need to think about how to develop it in code or any such things, just allow yourself to dream freely and pick an idea.

2. Identify the problem space and needs

After finding an idea for something you want to create, dive into this idea deeper. Imagine - or find out for real - the target user group of this product, app, or design.

What are the needs of these potential users? You can either do some real market research, or make up your imagined user group by assumptions and fantasy.

Your target user group probably has some specific characteristics, interests, needs, wants, and desires that you'll design for.

You can use these points to create personas, draw up potential user journeys, and use these points to empathize with them.

3. Create a design system or visual guidelines

If you want to, you can also practice creating your first simple [design system or visual guidelines](#) for projects. This can be good practice for future cases.

Think about what the target group might respond to for visual languages, such as colors, tone of the copy, how used they are to digital products, and so on.

Further in the process, you can use these guidelines for creating mockups and visual details.

4. Brainstorm, find inspiration, and sketch

As we've gone through in previous chapters on the design process, begin by brainstorming, finding inspiration, and sketching out various ideas.

Remember to take pictures or document the process along the way, so that you can use the material to put together a project for your portfolio or if you may want to present the design process to someone in the future.

Then, use those bases to create your first mockups and prototypes of an app, website, service, or product that can solve the problem or need you started out with.

5. Perform usability tests and get feedback

If you want to add an extra touch of user experience (UX) design, you can perform usability tests or evaluate your own design according to usability heuristics.

Another way is to ask for feedback from senior designers or post your design on social media to ask for feedback.

From these usability tests or other evaluations, create iterations of the design to improve it. This can also be documented, to show that you know how to iterate on design solutions.

You have now created a real design based on your own idea!

5.1.2. Putting it all together

Thereafter, you can collect your notes, personas, user journeys, visual guidelines, sketches, wireframes, mockups, and learnings into one file.

In this file, describe a narrative around your design process. Try to use proper methodology as well as your own words to describe the work process.

You can also include what software you used, how you evaluated your solutions, learnings from feedback or usability tests, and how you landed on the decisions that you did.

The file can be made and saved as a text document, PDF, video format, or a website, uploaded to Behance or Dribbble, or any other form you may feel comfortable with. From this, you now have a complete design project that you can showcase!

Design Portfolio
What to include and why

6. Build a Design Portfolio

Design is one of those skills that is best validated by showcasing previous work and creations, which is why it's important to have some sort of work portfolio.

6.1. What is a design portfolio?

A design portfolio is a collection highlighting your previous work, projects, and creations. It can be in the form of a website, pdf, or in physical format and is often required when applying for jobs.

A portfolio is both proof of your skills, as well as a way for you to present your work in your desired way.

For example, you can omit previous projects that you *do not* want to do more of and include projects which you do want to work with.

The way you showcase your projects also shapes the story you tell about your creative journey. It's a way for you to explain how your thought process goes and how you work.

Potential employers want to see if and how you can fit into their creative process, and your portfolio is a way for you to show that.

6.1.1. Which format to choose

As a UI designer, you may use social media such as Dribbble or Behance as a portfolio, but it's recommended to create your own portfolio website.

The reason it's good to create your own website is that UI design is closely tied to front-end development. By creating your own website, you're showing potential employers that you not only know design, but that you also understand the technical parts.

You can either code your website from the ground up or use CMS such as WordPress. Which one you decide on depends on your level of skill and ambition.

6.1.2. What to include

Design projects

Most importantly, your portfolio needs to contain your design projects. If you are a complete beginner, you may not have any projects to show, which is why your first task will be to create 2-4 UI designs.

The first projects you create can either be done solo as a passion project or together with a company, paid or unpaid.

If you have multiple projects, you may want to select a few of them that you are the proudest of, and that show potential employers or clients what you're looking more of doing.

When presenting your project, think about the story you want to tell. Include what the problem or vision was, and all the methods and steps you took in order to end up with your end design. Give context about time restrictions, who you worked with, and what your area of responsibility was.

These presentations of earlier projects will also help you in job interviews, where it is very common to get asked to talk about or present an earlier project you've done.

Resume

If you are looking to become employed, you can also include your resume on your portfolio website. This is not as necessary however if you're only looking for freelance projects, but it can help.

Personal projects

Apart from strictly professional projects or concepts, you may include personal projects, in particular, if you are looking for a more artistically creative role.

For example, showings additional skills in illustration, drawing, or writing makes you look more well-rounded, creative, and passionate. All of which are good qualities to have as a designer.

Contact information

Don't forget to include ways to get in contact with you. If a visitor enjoys what they see, you'll want to give them easy access to communicate with you. Include information such as your email, phone number, or social media.

Be mindful, however, if you include your social media, there is a possibility of employees looking at it and judging your professionalism on it.

What you can do to separate private life and work life is to create social media accounts specifically for your design projects.

Personality

A big part of being accepted and trusted is related to how others perceive us as people. Having your own space where you show off your work, also allows you to show your personality.

The tone of voice you use, the words you choose, colors, and so on, can all give a positive or negative first impression.

Think carefully about how your portfolio makes you look, and if it fits with how you want to be perceived.

Career

7. Career

UI design is an attractive career path not only because of its unique combination of art, design, and technology but also because it's one of the highest-paying creative fields.

Since UI design jobs are mostly within tech and IT departments, the booming tech salaries boost UI Designers' income compared to many other purely visual jobs. Because of this, the competition for jobs can be fierce, especially for beginners.

In this chapter, we're going to go through topics that are relevant to starting a career in UI design: education, landing your first job, freelance versus employment, possible career paths, and earning potential.

7.1. Education

Most UI designers learn design through one or a combination of formal education and self-taught.

Formal education is most commonly referred to as university degrees and other institutional certifications acknowledged by the industry to meet a certain quality standard and to follow an educational plan.

Self-taught, on the other hand, is learning through for example reading books and articles on your own, watching YouTube tutorials, taking online courses, private mentorship, and self-practicing.

Self-teaching may not follow a rigid educational plan but allows for more practical courses of action. There are pros and cons for each, which may be important to know before you decide on how to invest your time and money.

7.1.1 Formal education

Formal education is a structured and systematic way of learning, often helping up to certain standards. Most common examples or university programs and diplomas that are recognized by others.

These educational paths follow a certain curriculum, have dedicated mentors and teachers, and end with receiving formal certifications or degrees.

Pros of formal education
Credential/Signaling

Achieving degrees, diplomas, and certifications may seem unnecessary if you can learn the knowledge on your own. But truth is that most likely, having formal certifications can affect your status and "personal branding". Formal and recognized education can be status boosters and give you immediate credibility among those who recognize it.

Even if a company or the person hiring doesn't have formal education as a strict criterion, a degree or certification still signals to others that you have the skills and intelligence needed.

For some companies, an official university degree in a relevant subject is even a strict criterion. This is more common with bigger companies that get hundreds or even thousands of applicants, and choose to filter away candidates based on degrees.

If you don't have a degree, it may not matter how good you are or how much experience you have for these companies. So, if you plan on landing a job at a big company known for prioritizing formal education, you would do well to get one yourself.

Network and friends

Studying at a university or other type of institution with classmates and teachers whom you get to know throughout your education gives you a valuable network.

From your network of professional peers, you may find yourself receiving work opportunities you otherwise would have missed.

In addition, studying together with people who have similar interests and career goals is a great way to make lifelong friends or even find a partner. You'll easily connect based on shared experiences, memories, as well as interests.

Motivation

Studying in a learning environment such as an educational institute and being surrounded by others learning the same things and who are struggling with the same challenges can be motivating.

Our environment, both physical and the people we are surrounded by and their behavior, affects us. It can be much easier to stay focused, disciplined, and work towards your goals when you are surrounded by others with a similar mindset.

Specialist technical knowledge

The level of specialist technical knowledge acquired from formal education can be a unique advantage depending on your goals.

You might not need a Ph.D. in human-technology interaction to get a junior role as a UI Designer. But if you want to come up with incredibly innovative product ideas and designs, a Ph.D. might give you specialist knowledge that is very hard to come by through only self-studying.

Standard

Most formal educational programs have a set standard that students need to meet in order to pass courses or get degrees. This standard can make sure that you learn what you need to learn. It can also be beneficial in the way that others may judge your skills through it.

Cons of formal education
Costs

Formal education is often expensive, both the education in itself and the living costs and missed-opportunity costs. The costs may not always be worth it in terms of lost earnings per year compared to potential earnings over life, based on your age and current financial situation.

If you live in a country with free education, you can utilize that while working part-time to minimize the financial costs of education. If not, you can apply for scholarships and financial aid from different organizations to finance your studies, as well as save up well beforehand and set up plans to lower your living costs before you start studying.

Sacrifices

You may also need to make sacrifices in terms of geographical location, giving up current jobs or careers, and even relationships.

You can try to find an education that is remote, in order to stay at your current location. You can also try to negotiate with your current employer or clients about working part-time or remotely during your studies. Long-distance relationships may also work with mindful communication and by utilizing the internet.

The slow pace of learning

If you are a very fast learner, formal education may hinder the speed of your learning and force you to go slower than you are able to. Most teaching is standardized to fit the average student, but if you are more ambitious, passionate, and driven than that, it may instead drag you down.

Solution

Opt for self-studying in combination with formal education, you always have the opportunity to study more than your degree or certification requires.

You can also start doing your own UI design projects while still studying to build up a portfolio and personal brand during your studies.

7.1.2 Self-taught

Among UI Designers, there are many who are fully, or partially, self-taught. This is because UI design is still a fairly new discipline, and it takes time for new techniques and practices to get established in academia and then taught.

Frankly, UI design is a skill you certainly can learn on your own, even if the credentials of a formal education can help. If you feel that you would rather self-study, by all means, do it!

Methods

Self-learning can be achieved through means such as

- reading relevant books and articles
- watching tutorials and lectures online
- taking online courses
- learning from doing
- looking up curriculums for formal degrees and courses, and follow them on your own

Most people who decide to teach themselves do it for a real passion, which propels them to learn faster and more eagerly. It can also save you a lot of money, and allow you to tailor your education to your own interests.

Book recommendation

Don't Go Back to School - A Handbook for Learning Anything by Kio Stark

Pros of being self-taught

Cheaper

Self-studying is often cheaper, and could even be free. It's something you can do on the side as you have a full-time income from something else. This can provide safety and fit better for those who have financial obligations that are difficult to get away from.

Freedom & variety

Being self-taught also creates more freedom in what areas of knowledge you want to explore, and what types of information and projects you choose to engage in. It also isn't tied to a certain geographical area or specific people.

Real-world application

Being self-taught can result in learning more practical skills and real-world applications, compared to formal theoretical education such as university degrees.

Cons of being self-taught

Lack of guidance

Being self-taught requires knowledge about knowing *what* you need to learn, and how to learn it in the best way. When there's no one to guide you, you may accidentally miss important lessons or skip boring parts that would be beneficial for you to learn.

Follow a study program, guide, or educational book from start to finish. Do not skip parts. Ask for feedback from senior designers to pinpoint areas you may be lacking in.

May take longer

Learning without proper teachers and mentors may take longer since you may not know the most efficient way of studying, and you also may lack motivation and discipline.

Set a schedule, deadlines, and goals for yourself. You can take inspiration from the schedule of formal education. Many universities and courses publicly display their course plan and literature, which you can copy on your own.

Knowledge may not be recognized

Being entirely self-taught doesn't lead to any official certifications or degrees that are recognized by other people. This can be a struggle in the beginning and you may need to prove your skills and knowledge in other ways.

Prioritize creating a high-quality portfolio of your work and projects. Go to meetups, coworking places, and seminars where you can use social skills to get work opportunities. Be entrepreneurial, build a brand for yourself, and learn to market your skills through social media, a personal website, or an SEO Linkedin profile.

May automatically be filtered from application processes

Unfortunately, there are companies who will use software programs to automatically filter away all applications without formal education on their resume. This can be a huge disadvantage in getting your first job.

Solution

Seek work at smaller companies and startups that may not get as many applicants, and therefore may not be as picky. You can also try getting jobs by seeking out people personally through Linkedin or other social media, and avoid going through the usual route of applying.

7.2. How to Land Your First Job

There are many ways to land your first job. The most common way is to reach out to companies yourself, by applying for jobs. Another way is to attract companies and clients to reach out to you, through a personal website, and social media presence, and establish yourself as an expert.

As a beginner, you will most likely be the one who reaches out to companies, persuading them to give you a chance. When you get more experienced and build up your own reputation, you can market yourself to attract others to come to you.

My biggest recommendation to you on your first job is to approach it with the attitude of an apprentice. You are there to learn, develop, and gain experience. Don't be afraid to learn from others, perhaps find a mentor, and be willing to try new things and be helpful.

7.2.1. Portfolio

Before all else, as mentioned earlier, create a good portfolio that showcases your projects, skills, and earlier experiences. You'll need this.

It's through your portfolio that potential employers, clients, and colleagues can get proof of your actual skills and competencies, no matter if you have a formal education or not.

Read more about creating a portfolio in the [chapter about portfolios](#).

7.2.2. Job websites

There are many websites and social media sites such as LinkedIn and Indeed where companies and potential clients post available jobs. Through browsing these, you can apply by sending your CV and portfolio along with a personal letter.

Some design positions precisely mention "Junior" in the title or description, which means that they are looking for someone who doesn't have much experience yet. This is probably the type of position you'd want to apply to as a beginner.

However, do not be intimidated by job descriptions. Job descriptions are descriptions of the *ideal* candidate, but ideals are not the same as reality. Many people have landed jobs without hitting all the criteria.

As long as you have confidence in your skills, and know how to teach yourself what you need to learn, apply for the positions that interest you. The worst that can happen is that you get ignored or get a no - which is a natural part of the job search anyway.

Popular websites to find UI design work:
- LinkedIn
- Indeed
- Angel.co (Startup jobs)
- Weworkremotely.com (Remote jobs)
- Dribbble (Design jobs & freelance projects)

- Upwork (Freelance projects)
- Fiverr (Freelance projects)
- Toptal (Freelance projects)

7.2.3. Networking

Networking is another word for the connections you have and people with whom you are familiar. In your network of people, some may be able to assist you in landing your first job.

This can for example be a former teacher with ties to the industries, or a friend of a friend who works at a company that's currently hiring UI designers.

Networking can also mean going to meetups or other networking events, where the purpose is to gather those who seek services and those who can offer them.

Another modern way of making professional connections is to use social media such as Instagram to connect and get to know other designers. They may share job tips or openings at their companies before they get posted on job sites such as LinkedIn where the competition is higher.

7.2.4. Internships

In most skilled professions, internships have been a popular way to learn, and it's the same with UI design. Internships are positions at organizations, often time-limited, and that offer practical work experience related to one's career och study interests.

Apart from gaining work experience, one can make valuable connections, develop soft skills, and gain insight into how a business or industry works.

If you are unable to find a paying job, starting with internships can be a great way to build up skills and experience *until* you can find paid work. However, if you are at a level where you know you can create good things, don't shy away from applying to paid junior positions as well, where you will also learn, as well as get paid.

7.2.5. Consultant companies

Many graduates find their first jobs through consultant companies that have a great network of companies seeking to hire. Through them, you can relax while they find you work.

However, the drawback is that consultancy companies often get a percentage of what you're earning. It's up to you if you think it's worth it.

7.2.6. Social media

You can use social media to tell the world "Here I am, this is what I can do, approach me if you want to create something together" - It's a great tool for mass communication and outreach.

You don't need to use your personal social media accounts to advertise your design skills. Many, if not most, choose to create separate professional accounts to showcase their design skills and to connect with others who do the same.

Creating separate professional and personal accounts can also be a great way to use social media tailored to your personal or professional interests, without needing to share too much personal information with strangers and future colleagues.

Facebook

On Facebook, for example, there are many groups centered around UI design and work opportunities within UI design. You can post about your own situation there and make yourself available, and if you're lucky, someone who's hiring may see you.

Instagram

On Instagram, you can create a new profile specifically for UI design work, where you can share your designs, processes, and what you've learned, and build a following. There are hashtags you can use such as #uidesign, that you can use to make your posts appear to those who are interested in them.

Being seen, getting attention, and recognition for your design work and personality can lead to unforeseeable benefits. It may lead to someone finding you who needs your expertise or may lead to someone being extra interested in you in a job interview.

By following lots of other designers who have an active following, commenting, and engaging with the community, you may also stumble upon new opportunities and make new friends.

Gaining a following

Furthermore, if you are a talented visual designer, who posts a lot of your projects online and have knowledge of social media marketing, there's a high chance that you can gain a decent following. This is what many refer to as creating a personal brand as a creative professional.

Having many followers on your professional accounts can signal a social acknowledgment of your skills to potential employers, and either provide you with job opportunities or help you in the application process.

Do note that the number of followers of course does not accurately reflect a designer's true value and that many highly talented designers do not even have social media accounts. But there is no denying that in this modern digitalized world we live in, those who can utilize social media to their own advantage can gain a lot from doing so.

7.2.7. Personal website

Building a personal website or blog centered around UI design is a long game, but it is something that is invaluable once you've succeeded.

A successful personal design website can draw in an unlimited amount of job offers and freelance opportunities as well as other valuable human connections.

However, it often takes a long time and requires you to know how to create your own website, design it, create content, work on SEO content, and so on. All of these, however, are skills that make you even more valuable as a designer.

7.2.8. For self-taught designers

As a self-taught designer landing your first job without a formal degree or meeting all requirements takes a bit of audacity. You must be willing and have the confidence to convince an employer to take a chance on you and to believe in your competence and ability to learn.

Without a certification or formal diploma, you need to prove your knowledge and value in other ways. Take special care in creating a great portfolio and document your project and design process well.

If you can show in your portfolio that you have studied enough to know the theory, methodology, processes, and tools, then you don't need formal papers to prove it.

Having a strong social media presence or network of credible people who can vouch for you can also be extra beneficial since it can provide the social credibility that formal education otherwise offers.

You may also need to exaggerate your skills a bit, as said by the famous quote "Fake it until you make it". Although do be careful doing this since you might not want to outright lie and get a bad reputation for it.

But if you truly do believe that you have what it takes to do a great job and that you are capable of learning and contributing with what you say that you can, then don't undersell your value.

7.2.9. Start small

Truth is, it is much easier to land your first job working for a small, local, and growing company, compared to one of the world's biggest and most prestigious ones.

If your main aim is to learn, it doesn't matter exactly where you learn first, as long as you are developing your skills. You will learn a lot either way. It's more important to get your foot in the door first than to wait years for your big break.

The advantage of big companies is that they may have set up proper mentorship programs and systems for developing skills. This can be very beneficial but is by no means the only way to develop skills fast and properly - "Where there is a will, there is a way".

Although there are current norms, systems, and ways careers often take form - you also have the opportunity to do it your own way. And even though some traditional paths may be more recommended, who is to say that those are the most fun, enjoyable or fruitful ways? Things are constantly changing, and you are a free agent that can pave your own path in the world.

Once you have gained some experience, you'll have an easier time landing a position at a more prestigious organization anyway, if that is your goal.

7.3. Employment vs Freelance

One of the great aspects of being a digital designer is the freedom it can allow. UI Designers can absolutely find various work that allows for flexibility, remote work, and good pay - both in the forms of employment as well as through independent contracting.

There is of course a lot of competition among the top-paid, most flexible, and most enjoyable occupations or projects, especially since companies can source designers globally. With experience, your opportunities of landing better opportunities will increase - however it may not be as easy in the beginning.

For that reason, I recommend beginners first get employment at a company for a few years to gain the necessary experience, insight, and soft skills needed. Being a valuable designer is more than just being able to create mockups, it's much more about social skills and business thinking.

By first working as an employed designer, you can learn from more senior designers, as well as develop important people skills, and learn about the ins and outs of product development and how businesses function.

As a freelance designer, your design skills may even come secondary to your skills as a marketer, your branding, your social skill, negotiation skills, and your ability to present and argue for your case. These skills are necessary to find stable, lucrative, and good freelance projects.

What type of employment works best for you, depends on your unique personality and skills. Some people do not thrive in ordinary employment with too little freedom, and others cannot handle the uncertainty of freelancing.

Multiple skill sets
If you are a creative professional who works within multiple fields such as writing, design, photography, and programming, freelancing might be for you.

If you have a wide variety of skills, you can take on 3-4 different projects simultaneously, in different fields. This might be more stimulating for multifaceted professionals.

For those who aspire to become self-employed independent designers, knowing a variety of skills is also greatly beneficial. Developing specific niche skills (think of the "T-shaped" designer) in combination with that, is even smarter.

Further, the success of a product or business is a combination of many different aspects not limited to UI Design.

Other important skills are marketing, graphic design, content creation, copywriting, UX Design, development, and the right visions. It is clear that the more knowledge and skills one has, the more one can contribute.

7.3.1. Employment

There are many different forms of design teams and ways various companies work with UI design, which will influence what you learn and which skills you develop first.

In-house

Working in-house means that you are employed at a specific company, most often working with one product or chain of products. For example, being employed in-house at Spotify means that you work as a designer for Spotify and their products.

The pros of being employed in-house are that it allows you to really dive into a product for a long period of time - perhaps years, and really get to know the market, business, users, product, and processes.

It's a great way to start your career because you learn the ins and outs of how business and product development works.

Working in-house also has the benefit of teaching you how to work in interdisciplinary teams, how to work in iterations, and how product management and processes work.

Many times, the pace of work for an in-house designer is calmer, depending on the company's maturity. Deadlines may be set internally and the company's income may not depend on deadlines being met on time.

You may also have bigger opportunities to perform a variety of work tasks as an in-house designer, which can be beneficial for trying out different things. This is especially common if you are the sole designer at a company.

However, being the sole designer of a company as a beginner does also come with its challenges. You may for example not get a proper mentor or mentorship program at work, which can hinder your growth.

In such a case, I'd advise you to seek [mentorship](#) and design feedback from senior designers outside of the company.

Agency

An agency takes up work from various clients, similar to how a freelancer works, but in a larger business.

The pros of working at an agency are that there is more variety in the projects you get to work on, which can be a great eye-opener for a beginner.

You may also get to learn how to work with real deadlines and get to learn how to deal with client-facing projects, which are all valuable skills.

However, working at an agency may also be more stressful since you may not be working with a particular product or cross-functional team for a longer period of time. You may also not fully get insight into how product development works.

7.3.2. Freelance

Being a freelancer means being self-employed and essentially running your own business.

Freelancing involves not only creating designs, but also marketing your skills, finding new clients, being able to negotiate pay, chasing after payments (occasionally), and financial responsibilities.

Before making the jump to freelancing full-time, ask yourself if you are willing and able to run your own business. Only you can know what your personality is best fitted for.

The smartest way may also be to start freelancing on the side while keeping employment if you are unsure. You can then increasingly move over to self-employment while still having the safety of an ordinary job.

Remember to check in your job contract first though, if you are allowed to take on freelance work on the side as some companies forbid it.

Pros

Most freelancers have more to say about where, when, and how they work, meaning more freedom and flexibility than being employed. In many cases freelancing also means being able to charge higher rates.

Freelancing allows you to focus your career trajectory on the particular industry, niche, or region you want to build a professional network and credentials. You also have the possibility to build a portfolio of work more fitting to your personal interests.

Cons

Being self-employed comes with more responsibilities. You are responsible for bringing in clients and income, paying taxes, doing all the paperwork, or hiring someone to. You are responsible for your own pension savings, health insurance, and invoicing.

However, all of those things can either be learned or you can hire someone to help you perform those responsibilities. But you must be willing to learn to navigate those tasks in one way or another, or it won't be easy.

Freelancing also means possibly higher risks of being without income for periods of time. But even as an employed designer, you can get fired and have trouble finding new work.

So, it's really a question of your own ability to market yourself and your skills. Therefore, the most valuable skill to learn as an independent professional is business skills.

7.4. Career Paths

UI Designers have many possible career paths in front of them, and since it is a multidisciplinary field, one can also choose to pivot into other related areas.

Within UI design, you can choose to specialize in specific skills such as creating Design Systems, working with micro-interactions, and illustrations, or designing for specific types of devices such as mobile apps or TV apps.

You could also broaden your scope and become more of a generalist, Product Designer, and seek roles as a UX/UI designer or UI developer.

You could also aim to leave practical UI design work entirely, and become a team lead and project manager, dealing more with the entire design and development process.

As the tech field is still ever-changing, every couple of months or years new career paths take form. This means that you don't have to be defined by specific titles, but can invent your own.

If you choose to pursue a lifestyle of continuous learning, education, and acquiring new skills, you will find yourself naturally developing in a variety of directions. From a position of experience and a wide range of skills and experiences, you'll know even better which path to follow.

You do not have to feel tied to the identity of being a UI Designer, you can see it as a stepping stone to gaining the experiences and skills you need to create good things. After all, titles are just arbitrary, but your abilities are what's valuable.

7.5. How much do UI Designers earn?

No matter if you are going into UI design for passion or money, it's always smart to be aware of how the market looks like.

However, it is worth mentioning that the market salary for UI design varies by country, region, and local industry.

To find out which type of design work pays more, you can use services such as Glassdoor and Payscale. You can use this information to decide which specializations you want to niche down on, as well as utilize it for salary negotiations.

In general, the more experience you have the more you will get paid. In addition, the more unique but sought-after skillsets you have, the more you can get paid.

Currently, programmers get slightly higher than designers in tech, which leads to coding as a skill that can increase your earnings as a designer.

More responsibility often also leads to higher pay, which means that after a few years of experience, you could aim to become a design lead, manager, or director which typically pays more.

In general, you could also earn more by becoming an independent consultant or freelancer, setting your own rates. There is no real limit to how much you can work and earn, compared to how there often is a ceiling to salaries in employment.

If you choose this path in order to earn more, focus on your marketing skills, personal brand as an independent creative professional, as well as your network and reputation. All those things will help tremendously.

7.5.1. Passion vs money

As one of the most classic questions in regard to career choices follows: Should you go after what you enjoy the most or what pays the most?

The right answer to that question depends on your personality and your values. What do you think would make you happiest overall?

To enjoy what you're doing for work every day, with perhaps less money for materialistic consumptions and other experiences, or to not enjoy your days as much, but with more money to spend?

This question is more difficult if you're deciding between wildly different career choices with a wildly different income range. However, when it comes to deciding which niche or specialization to go for within UI design, the question becomes easier.

Even if there is a pay difference between UI Designers leaning towards either visual design, UX research, or front-end development, the difference won't be big enough to drastically change your lifestyle.

If you do something you are truly passionate about or have a natural tendency towards, chances are that you will become *really* good at it. If you get really great at something, chances are that you will be able to earn a lot of money from doing it.

Extremely skilled, talented, and passionate UI Designers in whichever specialization, are generally paid more than someone who is only mediocre or below average in another specialization.

So, it follows that it would be smart to specialize in whichever area you are most passionate about and talented in.

However, if you are not passionate about anything in particular, nor have any natural talents in any specific direction, then it makes more sense to go after what pays more.

Note, however, that skills in sales, marketing, networking, and social competence may in the end be more important determinators of your income and ability to earn than any specialization.

7.6. Confidence & Imposter Syndrome

Many young professionals struggle with the feeling of being inadequate to do the job one is hired for - even if there are no outside indicators of that. This phenomenon is called experiencing imposter syndrome.

Both junior and senior designers can experience imposter syndrome, and some may experience it their entire professional career. There are some tips that may help you get rid of, or at least soothe, this feeling.

Develop trust

Some people may experience imposter syndrome without any reason to - even if they are fully adequate to do the job. So, one way to help the situation is to develop trust that the people who hired you to do the job have done so for good reasons.

You have been given the chance to work with design since the people who have hired you have judged your character, education, and skills as proficient enough to do the work. Trust that.

You may also need to work on developing trust that the education, courses, books, and tutorials you've learned from have taught you what you need to know. In addition, trust your own ability to learn, develop, and think. What you don't know, you can learn.

Develop your skills

However, if you really are a beginner and your bad confidence is based on the fact that you actually don't have the skills you need to have, then the solution is simply to work on building strength in the areas you know you lack.

Spend time to reflect on which areas you are most insecure about, and why. Then, invest time and energy to improve your skills and knowledge in those areas.

For example, improve your skills and knowledge by educating yourself further, reading relevant books and articles, and asking more senior designers for tips.

A healthy dose of humbleness is good, and it is good to know your own limitations and weaknesses. However, going around with constant stress and anxiousness about your own abilities will affect your mental state negatively. So, don't be afraid to talk about it with others and reach out for help and support if you need it.

Local & Digital

Design Community

8. Design Community

There's an active global design community thanks to international travel as well as the internet.

As a beginner, it can be of great help to connect with fellow designers and working professionals all over the world, to get help, connect, make friends, and find inspiration.

Local community

Most cities also have a local community that you can meet through physical meetups and coworking spaces.

These physical meetups can be found through apps such as Meetup or Facebook groups dedicated to specific cities.

To find relevant Facebook groups, try searching for "[Your City] + UI Design" on Facebook. To find relevant meetups, try downloading the Meetup app and searching for events in your area.

Digital community

The global design community can also be easily accessed digitally on social media such as Facebook groups and Instagram, as well as specific social media such as Dribbble.com and Behance.net.

Instagram is also a great platform for designers because it's graphic-based and you can comment and send DMs. You can find the UI design community through hashtags such as #uidesign, #userinterface, and #uiinspiration.

9. Social Media & Websites

There are many dedicated social media sites and other websites where you can find lots of design inspiration.

The two most prominent social media networks that I'd recommend you to check out are dribbble.com and behance.net.

Other useful and inspirational resources:

- Figma community files - See all community files from Figma users
- Muzli - Get design inspiration when you open new tabs
- Awwwards - Discover award-winning designs
- UI Jar
- Collect UI
- Dark Mode Design
- Product Hunt

In addition, there are lots of personal blogs that write about design, more than could be counted. If you're interested, I have written a bunch of [articles about UI design](#) on my website as well.

Further Reading

10. References & Further Reading

This book has been created to be introductory and to give a way in for new designers. However, there is an endless sea of valuable information to take part in that could not be fit into one book.

For your further curiosity and education, I have gathered here the resources, references, and recommendations of books and articles to read.

Apart from these recommendations, don't forget that there is always a great amount of free information available at your fingertips, only a quick Google search away.

10.1. Books

Usability

- Don't Make Me Think by Steve Krug

- The Design of Everyday Things by Don Norman
- Rocket Surgery Made Easy by Steve Krug

Methods

- About Face: The Essentials of Interaction Design by Alan Cooper
- The Elements of User Experience by Jesse James Garrett
- Atomic Design by Brad Frost

Front-end development & design

- Refactoring UI by Adam Wathan & Steve Schoger
- HTML & CSS by Jon Duckett
- JavaScript and JQuery by Jon Duckett
- Thinking with Type by Ellen Lupton

Mindset

- Steal Like an Artist by Austin Kleo
- Show Your Work! by Austin Kleo
- Don't Go Back to School - A Handbook for learning anything by Kio Stark

10.2. Websites & Articles

Websites

- Nielsen Norman Group - nngroup.com
- Interaction Design Foundation - interaction-design.org
- UX Planet - uxplanet.org
- Baymard Institute Blog - baymard.com/blog
- Smashing Magazine - www.smashingmagazine.com
- UX Collective - uxdesign.cc

Articles: Usability

- 10 Usability Heuristics for User Interface Design - NN Group
- When to Use Which User-Experience Research Methods - NN Group
- Usability 101: Introduction to Usability - NN Group
- Heuristic Evaluation In UX Design: The Complete Guide - Career Foundry

Articles: Design Mindset

- Design Thinking 101 - NN Group
- The 5 Stages in the Design Thinking Process I IxDF - InxDF

Articles: UI Design

- Checkboxes vs. Radio Buttons - NN Group
- Personas – A Simple Introduction - InxDF

- [Designing The Perfect Slider UX](#) - Smashing Magazine

Check out my website for the next book!

www.ingramcontent.com/pod-product-compliance
Lightning Source LLC
LaVergne TN
LVHW051640050326
832903LV00022B/825